Tangible Terrain

poems by

Christy Wise

Finishing Line Press
Georgetown, Kentucky

Tangible Terrain

ACKNOWLEDGMENTS

These poems first appeared, sometimes in different forms, in the following
journals. Thank you to the editors of these journals:

Cathesix Northwest Press: "Ready" (published as "Last Day of Prophecy
Season")
Marin Poetry Center Anthology: "Ready" (published as "In the Gray")
Panoply, a literary zine: "Wolf call"
Red Flag Poetry—Poetry Express: "Biologist in Bliss"
SPANK the CARP: "Leap!"
Woodcrest Literary Magazine: "Gold, Dust"

Publisher: Leah Huete de Maines
Editor: Christen Kincaid
Cover Art: © Kathleen Lipinski
Author Photo: Elizabeth Dranitzke
Cover Design: Elizabeth Maines McCleavy

Order online: www.finishinglinepress.com
also available on amazon.com

Author inquiries and mail orders:
Finishing Line Press
PO Box 1626
Georgetown, Kentucky 40324
USA

Contents

In memory of my father,
with love

MY FATHER'S CITY
June 20, 2000

Eppler's Bakery on New Montgomery, half a block from where Dad spent weekdays. As I sat eating a sandwich outside today, scanning a barely recognizable (to me) San Francisco skyline, I thought about how much Dad loved San Francisco. I had attributed his decision to stay here, turning down geographic transfers and professional advancements, to a desire to stay in a gay-friendly city.

At that moment, I allowed myself to see another truth. And that is to understand his holistic love for this alabaster city.

THE VACANT LOT
aka The Field

I am a journalist,
a man of words,
yet I remain silent about the war.

My ten-year old son
                        and his buddies
create Germany's open fields
from a nearby scrubby vacant lot.

Plastic helmets,
toy machine guns,
tanks
props
playing Army.
That's what they call it.
Playing Army.

My war was not a game
but I am curious
                        about their curiosity.

Lucky to be alive is how I feel.
Fred didn't come back.
Sam's left ear no longer exists.
Larry's wife left him.

Dachau. We stumbled
into it.
How to describe

wretchedness?

My war was not a game
but I am curious

about their curiosity.

INVENTORY

Dad teaches me to cup
a blackberry
with my fingertips,
gently persuade release from stem.

Dad believes in a correct way to pick blackberries
like he has a method to roast marshmallows,
and shell Dungeness crab.
We work bushes

along railroad tracks, plentiful with berries.
A dark mound grows in the green plastic
bucket, one we use to create sandcastles at Santa Cruz.

Dad's silence
as we wander among prickly bushes
avoid ubiquitous bees
seems natural
not like long silences over dinner

which make me invisible.

I slip a few berries in my mouth
when Dad isn't looking.
He intends enough berries
for two pies and morning pancakes.

MT. TAMALPAIS

I lived at your feet when I was new,
unaware of your shelter.

As I grew I watched every day

assured of your constancy. Velvet
green crevices, small peaks
folded into each other with grace.

Later, I drove your inclines, one hairpin
after another. Etched into memory
from frequency, the curves a familiar dance.

I climbed up and over you
to swim the Pacific with friends,
or sit on sand
alone.
Sometimes there was sun.

Early mornings I hiked to the fire lookout,
watched sun emerge from behind Mount Diablo,
golden light so bright, I squinted to look.

From home, most evenings, fog veiled
my view, but I knew
                  you hadn't left me.

MOM SAID SHE WANTED ME TO LEARN FRENCH

I have a friend who speaks French, Mom said.
It's fun to learn a new language. Do you want to try?

Edith and I gathered Wednesday afternoons in her garden,
ate fresh cut apples and toasted almonds while I acquired
French words for things surrounding us.

pomme
amande
coquelicot
gros rocher

Edith survived foot passage over Swiss peaks,
escaped from Nazis, trekked without complaint,
vowed she would tell her grandchildren
how hunger haunted her steps.

She refused to let her mind go dark with thoughts
of death. I learned about Edith's story from Mom.
I didn't know how to discuss it with Edith.

We giggled when her cocker spaniel burrowed
beneath daisies to capture a stray almond.
Le chien est fou.

I loved him as much as I loved Edith.

IN SEPIA

My father, at 21, surrounded by five college
friends, reporters and editors, working
on the campus newspaper.

In sepia photo, one poises fingers over a typewriter,
another drapes his legs sideways over a chair, argyle
vests, wire-rimmed glasses, smiles. It's 1943.

Later, after dropping galleys at the printer,
they share pitchers of beer at the O, victorious
at making deadline. Voices drop decibels
when Europe edges into conversation.

College years about to be stolen. For some, lives.
Gallows humor keeps ghosts at bay during daylight.
At 2 AM, spirits scream.

Darkness offers one comfort: each other.
Men slip into night
alone
rendezvous in pairs
into shared beds.

OURS TO TAKE

Noisy, mysterious, full of pollywogs,
frogs, pussy willows,
bulrushes, The Swamp
our hideout from the confusing adult world.

The Swamp created a clearing between
a small dairy farm owned by a Portuguese family
and a eucalyptus grove near our house.

I heard Barn owls call from inside the grove
while I tried to fall asleep.

We created pollywog ecosystems
with four inches of water in mayonnaise
jars that we carried home and watched,
waiting for legs to sprout.
Few survived.

Even in third grade, we were conquerors
intent on capturing what we discovered. Many times,
we explored The Swamp without jars, crawled
for hours among reeds, cattails.

Still, we knew the marsh was ours,
not just to investigate.
But to take.

MY FATHER'S CITY—PART TWO
June 20, 2000

Dad spent lunch hours walking through the City. He
knew its neighborhoods, reported on the waterfront,
was active in the Press Club.

This was his City and he reveled in it. He knew
the secrets of its delicious coffee. Add a touch of powdered
chocolate to the top of the grounds before brewing a large
pot. He was pleased to have enticed that knowledge from a
prominent restaurateur.

NIGHTFALL

In the Great Depression, Dad's father lost
his job. Then, the house. Grandma returned
to nursing; Grandpa struggled to mask shame.

Stocks invested by Mom's grandfather
became worthless.

Destroyed, too: optimism.
A few years later, Mom found his body
hanging from the crossbeam of his carpentry workshop.

Perhaps my parents could not fathom
bedtime fears of a young girl
who lived in a comfortable home
a half mile walk to a good public school.

Perhaps.

Nightly drinking
sequestered
in the living room
prevented them
from taking time to tuck me in
kiss me goodnight,
wish sweet dreams.

READY

The sun rises when she feels good and ready.
We live at her mercy.

Good and ready. Strange phrase.
Ready seems straightforward but *good*?
What is it for the sun to be good?

Her performance is rising.
She brings daylight, sustenance.

No days off.
She departs at dusk.
Visits our kin
in another hemisphere.

What about a cloudy day?
Gray territory.
Is she deciding whether to be good?
Getting ready?

Sun: I'm sleeping in today. It's my birthday.

World: Your birthday? You know your birthday?

Sun: It's Miranda Legato 5479. And that's today.

World: How old are you?

Sun: 4.603 billion years, give or take. But this is the day I was born. I have another five billion years to go, give or take. I'm good. I'm ready.

ALL MINE

Grandma bought pretty skirts, soft sweaters
during my summer visits. She wanted
me to have new clothes for school's start.

Bridge partners, gardening chums knew
not to call during my week with Grandma.
If we ran into a friend, she introduced me like royalty.

We paused at lunchtime for a sandwich, potato chips
and fruit. The best part: an Eskimo pie.

We read in afternoons or she watched me swim
with cousin Rob at Hiram Johnson pool. Iced tea,
lemonade late afternoon, then a walk around the block.

When Grandpa came home, they shared a drink
under trellised grape vines that sheltered us
from Central Valley heat. I recounted our adventures.

Time with Grandma was fluid
because hers was all mine.

LEAP!

To take hold
like a frog in a storm
clutching a low branch
muddy river rushing below
moving too swiftly for swimming
shore too distant to leap.

      To take hold
      frog   storm
      clutching   branch
      river rushing
      moving swiftly swim
      shore   distant   leap.

           Take hold!
                 Storm
          Clutch
                   Rush
           Move   Swift
                   Swim
            Shore   Distant
                            Leap!

MY FATHER'S CITY—PART THREE

June 20, 2000

Dad came to the City from college, having experienced a dark side of humanity, fighting in Europe in World War II.

Like many veterans who survived, he returned to school. Books report that older vets were more serious about their educations and hurried to finish. I don't have that impression about Dad. It seemed he was glad to be back, had fun working on the Daily that year.

After graduation, he roomed with a couple of friends, embraced this life, his life. It was a carefree time. Great to be back in the U.S, among friends, to be alive, living in a beautiful place, doing work he loved.

BIOLOGIST IN BLISS

I met a plant biologist in Bliss,
Idaho at the Cloud Nine Café. He cruised
the West in a rusty Chevy pickup.

He subsisted in Bliss longer than wished.
Truck's transmission, trashed,
biologist, short on cash.

Strange name for a town, he sniffed.
Maybe then, it was blissful, I said.
I doubt it, he dissed.

We kissed a bit; danced around
a romance. I was passing through.

Spent a couple days up to my chin
in steaming water, then blitzed
out of Bliss.

I want to believe biologist
broke free, found
Rapture in Indiana.

WAIT. RETRIEVE. TOSS. DRAG.

Four apple varieties: one trunk!
Tree thrives.
Perfect location.

Mom and Dad admire our multi-grafted tree.

Golden delicious, Fuji, Granny Smith, Gala
sweeten autumns, provide sustenance
school lunches, fill Mom's pies, pancakes.

Family pruning day in February is mandatory.
That morning, Dad devours his usual poached eggs
and toast, wears frayed khakis, ripped white t-shirt.

Shears tucked into belt, Dad places
ladder, just so. My brother, Jeff,
and I stand nearby, ready.
Mom: alert for anything, everything.

Pruning Day is about waiting.
Wait while Mom and Dad discuss cuts.
Wait for branches to fall.
Retrieve branches.
Toss onto tarp.
Drag to vacant lot.
Wait.
　　　　Retrieve.
　　　　　　　Toss.
　　　　　　　　　　Drag.

Jeff and I crack jokes, belittle Dad's fastidiousness.

Stop that, kids!
Pay attention.

Within an hour, Jeff and I plot escape.
Tree half-shaggy, Dad recognizes futility.

Skedaddle, you two! We'll finish up.

He is tired, too. Perhaps he longs
for our saggy couch, a book.
But, like many
of his generation
he doesn't walk from a task,
unfinished.

Wait
         retrieve
                toss
                         drag.

THE FIELD

Tall straw grasses hide an occasional garter snake,
blue belly lizard. Robins perch on stout stalks,
alert for grasshoppers. The Field stretches for miles,
we think. In reality, it is the last vacant lot.

Hours spent there might tally years. Mom commands
us home, two houses away, another side of the world,
with a cow bell. That means dinner or come in for the night.

Bulldozers arrive. Loud motors, blades, thick tires
churn up the land. We are outraged, powerless. Adults
inflict irrevocable damage, we learn.

That dark scything summer
we could have constructed new forts
on hills farther away, or fished for crawdads
in the bay. We sulked,
seethed, grieved.

The three McCleary boys who move into the new house
don't stand a chance.
We hate them before they arrive
and never stop cursing.

CLOSED CLOSET: 1964

Dave and Fred
live together as a couple
not exactly open at the office,
but not secret socially

not deep in the closet like a lost shoe
or that dead turtle I found in my loafer last week
a refugee from my son's room
who walked pretty far for a pet turtle
but after a day or so,
ended up dead from dehydration and hunger.

GOLD, DUST

The Gold Rush wanes
by the time two brothers
reach northern California.

It will last forever. Visions of free
shiny flakes glittering in foothill streams sustain
them for four brutal months of travels

What is the price of leaving wives, children
on Prince Edward Island?
Cost of gangrene from axe injury?
Tab of heavy drinking, knife fights?

It's the rush. Gold glints in creek beds.
$16 to $20 a day. Fast money, always a rush,
the rush of being flush.

The two Irishmen straggle into Placerville.
Trash mounds higher than wagon roofs, abandoned
shanties. Scrawny pack mules pick at garbage, gravel.

They will not return East.
They lack fortitude for another crossing,
no gold to pay the way.

Not risk-takers by nature, they reclaim
laborer roots, travel
to the Central Valley, work wheat fields.

They don't speak of failure or regret,
but each morning brings dread about the day
ahead, and the next one after that.

They rush nowhere. Not even sun is golden.

MY FATHER'S CITY—PART FOUR
June 20, 2000

There was a fun-loving side to Dad, a wicked sense of humor, appreciation for music, art, gardening, good food, that got a bit lost in later years as alcoholism took over.

Disappointments about what didn't happen in his life accumulated.

I realize I'm doing a stereotypical thing of piecing together my father's life after he's gone. I guess it's a rite of passage. I'm no different.

WOLF CALL

In muted,
silvery dawn
haunting,
            forceful howl

reverberates
across snowy canyons,

emerges
wild,
from ancient place

dominant, singular
in January

grizzlies in hibernation.

HOME

Randy lives on a vacant lot near Walmart,
        names it his redwood forest.
lives in a Perkins moving box;
        his cottage.
He dines off an overturned milk crate;
        his rustic table.
eats hamburger scraps from Mel's;
        his nightly feast.
sleeps under a scratchy wool blanket;
        his comforter.

People call him crazy, but Randy knows

        to imagine
        is to survive.

GRANDPA'S PIGGY BANK

Size of my clenched fist, the pottery
piggy bank survived San Francisco's
1906 earthquake and fire.

Grandpa was ten when his family
fled their flat from uncontrolled fire,
took refuge at Mission Dolores cemetery.

His mother told her three children
wear as many clothes as possible,
leave everything else.

Grandpa's father wasn't home the night before
didn't return for about a week.
His girlfriend lived across town.

A tent settlement became the family's home.
Fire for three days, three nights.
On the fourth day, Grandpa sneaked back

and found his ceramic piggy bank nestled
among warm ashes, intact. A small chip
on its left ear revealed beige stoneware.

From flames, the pig's ocean blue glaze
became a swirl of black and navy, the surface
remained shiny and smooth.

Grandpa's coins safe inside, earnings
from errands and odd jobs for neighbors.
Grandpa tucked the pig into his corduroy jacket.

Safe in the family's tent, Grandpa curled up
on a blanket in the corner, cradled his pig.

TANGIBLE TERRAIN

Grandma knew weather.
She grew up on a family soybean farm
near Rensselaer, Indiana.
She knew weather.

Make hay while the sun shines
was more than a catchy axiom.
When sun broke between rainy spells,
haymakers rolled out of the barn.

Weather set plans for furrowing, planting,
hay-making, fertilizing. Dearth of rain, worse.
Even decades later, when Grandma noticed
impending drought, she felt the weight.

They only talk about the weather.
Mom scoffed at Dad and Grandma's
Sunday night calls. I shrugged.
Harmless topic.

What did Mom want them to discuss?
They couldn't unwind the once spoken,
thoroughly rejected, perpetually ignored.

Weather was incontrovertible
between Grandma and Dad.
A safe landing for both.

WISDOM LIKE BOSS

From The Reivers (movie)

Survival was outdoors,
out of my suburban house
ominous silence, spitfire tempers
which felt like my fault
though I was invisible.

I could breathe
among eucalyptus groves
that sheltered frogs in the swamp

or dunk my hands in brackish wetlands,
scooping up clams.

We didn't fear death, in those days, because we believed
that your outside was just what you lived in and slept
in and had no connection to what you were.

Ah, for wisdom like Boss in *The Reivers.*
To say to myself as a little girl:

Let all this wash over you.
a granite boulder
in the middle of
Feather River, churning
after a storm.

Christy Wise's poems and essays can be found in *Red Flag Poetry, Bayou Magazine, The Dewdrop, SPANK the CARP Anthology 2022* and *Upside Down and From Below*, Marin Poetry Center Anthology 2020.

Her poem "Tony's Cocoon" was a finalist in the Julia Darling Memorial Poetry Prize. Christy's essay "Memory Book" was designated a notable essay in *Best American Essays of 2010*.

With her mother, Nancy Baker Wise, Christy co-authored *A Mouthful of Rivets: Women at Work in World War II*, oral histories by women employed in non-traditional jobs during the Second World War.

Fourth-generation Californian, Christy cherishes walks along the Pacific Ocean and hikes in Desolation Wilderness.

www.ingramcontent.com/pod-product-compliance
Lightning Source LLC
Chambersburg PA
CBHW022100080426
42734CB00009B/1428